His & Hers

Compiled by
NORMAN
COLUMBIA
and
ELIZABETH KRASS

 STANYAN BOOKS

 RANDOM HOUSE

A Stanyan Book
Published by Stanyan Books,
8721 Sunset Blvd., Suite C
Hollywood, California 90069
and by Random House, Inc.
201 East 50th Street,
New York, N.Y. 10022

Printed in U.S.A.

Designed by Hy Fujita

Library of Congress Catalog
Card Number: 72-81613

ISBN: 0-394-48215-8

HIS & HERS

When Adam was lonely,
God created for him
not ten friends, but one wife.

— Chad Varah

Women are the sex which
believes that if you charge it,
it's not spending; and if
you add a cherry to it,
it's not intoxicating.

— *Bill Vaughan*

Being a woman is a terribly difficult
task since it consists principally
in dealing with men.

— *Joseph Conrad*

According to the Bible,
woman was the last thing
God made.
It must have been a Saturday night.
Clearly, he was tired.

—*Alexandre Dumas* (fils)

It is a truth universally acknowledged, that a single man in possession of a good fortune, must be in want of a wife.

— *Jane Austen*

I should like to see any kind of
a man, distinguishable from
a gorilla, that some good and even
pretty woman could not shape
a husband out of.

—*Oliver Wendell Holmes*

She is a woman,
therefore may be woo'd; She is a woman,
therefore may be won.

— *William Shakespeare*

Let men tremble to win the hand of
a woman, unless they win along with
it the utmost passion of her heart.

— *Nathaniel Hawthorne*

Woman would be more charming if
one could fall into her arms
without falling into her hands.

— *Ambrose Bierce*

Where lives the man
that has not tried
How mirth can into folly glide,
And folly into sin!

— *Sir Walter Scott*

Men do not think
Of sons and daughters, when
they fall in love.

— *Elizabeth Barrett Browning*

No matter how hard a man may labour,
some woman is always in the
background of his mind.
She is the one reward of virtue.

— *Gertrude Atherton*

Every man who is high up loves
to think he has done it all
himself; and the wife smiles, and
lets it go at that. It's our
joke. Every woman knows that.

— *James Barrie*
What Every Woman Knows

A woman's advice has little value,
but he who won't take it is a fool.

— *Cervantes*

Woman's counsel is full often fatal.

— *Chaucer*

Where women are, the better
things are implied if not spoken.

— *Amos B. Alcott*

No more subtle master under heaven
Than is the maiden pleasure for a
maid, Not only to keep down the
base in man
But teach high thought,
and amiable words
And courtliness, and the
desire of fame
And love of truth, and
all that makes a man.

— *Alfred, Lord Tennyson*

If the heart of man is depress'd
with cares, The mist is dispell'd
when a woman appears.

— *John Gay*

A man who has no office to go to—I don't care who he is— is a trial of which you can have no conception.

— *George Bernard Shaw*

My wife's gone to the country,
Hurray, hurray!
She thought it best; I need a rest,
That's why she went away.

— *George Whiting and Irving Berlin*

Wretched is the dame to whom the sound, "Your lord will soon return," no pleasure brings.

—*Maturin*

Suffer women to arrive at an
equality with you, and they will
from that moment become
your superiors.

— *Cato the Elder*

Ye must know that women have
dominion over you: do ye not labour
and toil, and give and bring
all to the woman?

— The Apocrypha, *IV, 22.*

She who ne'er answers till a
husband cools,
Or if she rules him,
never shows she rules.

— *Alexander Pope*

Along about 1960 a reporter from the *London Standard* demanded of Sir Winston Churchill, "What do you say, sir, to the prediction that in the year 2000, women will be ruling the entire world?"

Sir Winston raised a quizzical eyebrow and murmured, "They still will, eh?"

When you educate a man you educate an individual. When you educate a woman you educate a whole family.

— *Dr. Charles McIver*

A *free* man is a noble being; a *free* woman is a contemptible being… The use of this one word, in its two-fold application to men and women, reveals the unconscious but ever present conviction in the public mind that men tend, of course, heavenward in their natures and development, and that women tend just as naturally hellward.

— *Victoria Woodhull and Tennessee Claflin*

It is high time we stopped telling
children that girls don't have
the aptitude for mathematics,
engineering, science, etc. Most
girls are still raised with a
romantic idea of life—school,
marriage, family—and they
live happily ever after. But
Cinderella is dead!

—*Brig. Gen. Jeanne M. Holm*

If men and women are to understand
each other, to enter into each
other's nature with mutual sympathy,
and to become capable of genuine
comradeship, the foundation must
be laid in youth.

—*Havelock Ellis*

Marrying a woman because you
happen to be in love with her
is about as logical a proceeding as
throwing the cat out of the window
because the rhododendrons
are in bloom.

— *James Branch Cabell*

I cannot advise anyone to enter
into a marriage, sanctioned by the
civil law which continues to
support the dependence,
inferiority and social nullity
of the woman.

— *George Sand*

Man has found remedies against
all poisonous creatures, but
none was yet found against a
bad wife.

—*François Rabelais*

O sister sister! if ever you marry,
beware of a sullen, silent sot,
the one that's always musing but
never thinks. There's some
diversion in talking to a blockhead;
and since a woman must wear
chains, I would have the pleasure
of hearing 'em rattle a little.

— *George Farquhar*

If woman lost us Eden,
such as she alone can restore it.

— *John Greenleaf Whittier*

The woman tempted me —
and tempts me still!
Lord God, I pray you that she ever will.

— *Edmund Vance Cooke*

To put a tempting face aside
when duty demands every faculty…
is a lesson which takes most men
longest to learn.

— *Gertrude Atherton*

O woman! lovely woman!
Nature made thee to temper man:
we had been brutes without you!

— *Thomas Otway*

Men's weaknesses are often
necessary to the purposes of life.

— *Maurice Maeterlinck*

A man in general is better pleased
when he has a good dinner
upon his table, than when his
wife speaks Greek.

— *Samuel Johnson*

For a man seldom thinks
with more earnestness of anything
than he does of his dinner.

— *Piozzi*
Anecdotes of Samuel Johnson

Feed the brute.

— *George Du Maurier*
(Prescription for keeping
a husband's love, in Punch, *1886)*

Wives are young men's mistresses,
companions for middle age,
and old men's nurses.

— *Francis Bacon*

The air of the fireside withers out
all the fine wildings of the
husband's heart. He is so
comfortable and happy that he
begins to prefer comfort and
happiness to everything else on
earth—his wife included.

— *Robert Louis Stevenson*

We're all so—made so—'tis our
woman's trade
to suffer torment for
another's ease.

— *Elizabeth Barrett Browning*

It's my old girl that advises. She has
the head. But I never own to it
before her. Discipline must
be maintained.

— *Charles Dickens*
Bleak House

All you have to do, dearie, is think
up what's right — and let him
think *he* thought of it.

— *Alice Cass*
(Letters To My Daughter *1898*)

I find my wife has something in her
gizzard that only wants an
opportunity of being provoked
to bring up.

— *Samuel Pepys*

Men tell us what they think;
that is, what is right.
Why, then, must we keep silent
about our own thoughts?

— *Susan B. Anthony*

The woman was not taken
From Adam's head, you know,
So she must not command him,
'Tis evidently so;
The woman was not taken
From Adam's feet, you see,
So he must not abuse her—
The meaning seems to be.
The woman she was taken
From under Adam's arm
Which shows he must protect her
From injury and harm.

— Old Scots nuptial song

The talk of sheltering woman from
the fierce storms of life is the
sheerest mockery, for they beat
on her from every point of the
compass, just as they do on man,
and with more fatal results, for
he has been trained to protect
himself, to resist, to conquer.

—Elizabeth Cady Stanton

To be a woman is something so strange, so confusing and so complicated that only a woman could put up with it.

— Sören Kierkegaard

There is no other purgatory
but a woman.

— *Beaumont and Fletcher*

I had rather live with the woman
I love in a world full of trouble
than to live in heaven with
nobody but men.

— *Robert G. Ingersoll*

'Tis strange what a man may do
and a woman yet think him
an angel.

— *William Thackeray*

No woman is an absolute fool ... No
woman is ever completely deceived.

— *Joseph Conrad*

A wise woman never yields by
appointment. It should always be
an unforeseen happiness.

— *Stendahl*

Men, some to business, some to
pleasure take;
But every woman is
at heart a rake.

— *Alexander Pope*

What will not woman,
gentle woman dare
When strong affection
stirs her spirit up?

— *Robert Southey*

We shall find no fiend in hell
can match the fury of a
disappointed woman.

— *Colley Cibber*

When lovely woman stoops to folly,
And finds too late that men betray,
What charm can soothe her melancholy?
What art can wash her guilt away?

— *Oliver Goldsmith*

Some pray to marry the man they love,
My prayer will somewhat vary:
I humbly pray to Heaven above
That I love the man I marry.

— *Rose Stokes*

I have loved many, the more
and the few —
I have loved many,
that I might love you.

— *Grace Norton*

The man she had was kind and clean
And well enough for every day,
But, oh, dear friends,
you should have seen
The one that got away!

— *Dorothy Parker*

Such a clatter of words pours from
her tongue that you would
think all the pots and bells were
being clashed together.

— *Juvenal*

The sweetest noise on earth,
a woman's tongue;
A string which hath no discord.

—*Bryan Procter*

I am very fond of the company of
ladies. I like their beauty, I like
their delicacy, I like their vivacity,
and I like their silence.

—*Samuel Johnson*

The natural man has only two primal
passions, to get and to beget.

— *Sir William Osler*

What is man, when you come to
think upon him, but a minutely set,
ingenious machine for turning,
with infinite artfulness, the
red wine of Shiraz into urine?

— *Isak Dinesen*

Women's intuition is the result of millions of years of not thinking.

—*Rupert Hughes*

She can be as wise as we,
And wiser when she wishes.

—*George Meredith*

Women never use their intelligence—except when they need to prop up their intuition.

—*Jacques Deval*

Women are wiser than men because they know less and understand more.

—*James Stephens*

There is a tide in the affairs of women which, taken at the flood, leads—God knows where.

—Lord Byron

Women reason with the heart and are much less often wrong than men, who reason with the head.

—Marquis de Lescure

When I say I know women, I mean I know that I don't know them.

—William M. Thackeray

A woman's guess is much more accurate than a man's certainty.

—Rudyard Kipling

Every woman should marry—and no man.

— Benjamin Disraeli

Remember, it's as easy to marry a rich woman as a poor woman.

—William Thackeray

Marriage is a romance in which the hero disappears in the first chapter.

— Kathryn Maye

When singleness is bliss,
it's folly to be wives.

—*Bill Counselman*
Ella Cinders

Women, deceived by men, want
to marry them. It is a kind of
revenge as good as any other.

—*Phillippe de Remi Beaumanoir*

Many a marriage hardly differs
from prostitution, except being
harder to escape from.

—*Bertrand Russell*

Manner, not gold,
is woman's best adornment.

— *Menander*

For courtesy wins women
all as well as valor may.

— *Alfred, Lord Tennyson*

Tact is the saving virtue without
which no woman can be a success.

— *Sir William Osler*

Where there is neither love
nor hatred in the game,
woman's play is mediocre.

— *Friedrich Nietzsche*

Every man, as the saying is, can
tame a shrew but he that hath her.

— *Robert Burton*

The reason firm, the temperate will,
Endurance, foresight, strength, and skill;
A perfect woman, nobly planned,
To warn, to comfort and command.

—*William Wordsworth*

The appearance of things to the
mind is the standard of
every action to man.

— Epictetus

She must be seen to be appreciated.

—William Ainsworth

A modest woman, dressed out in all
her finery, is the most tremendous
object of the whole creation.

— Oliver Goldsmith

I...chose my wife, as she did her
wedding-gown, not for a fine
glossy surface, but such qualities
as would wear well.

— *Oliver Goldsmith*

Whenever a man's friends begin to
compliment him about looking
young, he may be sure that
they think he is growing old.

— *Washington Irving*

The same old charitable lie
Repeated as the years scoot by
Perpetually makes a hit —
"You really haven't changed a bit."

— *Margaret Fishback*

I have everything I had twenty
years ago, only it's all a
little bit lower.

— *Gypsy Rose Lee*

Making love to a woman too
many times is like
scratching a place that doesn't
itch any more.

— More Playboy's Party Jokes

As lovers, men are inclined to
be general practitioners
rather than specialists.

— *Helen Rowland*

Men have a better sense of
humor than women.

— *Bill Cosby*

*When asked by a man why
women lack a sense of humor:*

God did it on purpose, so that
we may love you men
instead of laughing at you.

— *Mrs. Patrick Campbell*

Nothing spoils a romance so much
as a sense of humor in the woman.

— *Oscar Wilde*

Oh, there are many things that
women know,
That no one tells them,
no one needs to tell.

— *Roselle Montgomery*

To our sweethearts and wives.
May they never meet.

— *A toast*

The really maddening thing about
unfaithful husbands is not so
much their infidelity as their smug
self-assurance that the wives
don't know.
Of *course* the wives know.

— *Anne Herschman*

Woman's love is but a blast,
And turneth like the wind.

— Sir Thomas Wyatt

The love of man? Exotic flower,
Broken, crushed, within an hour.
The love of woman?
Storm-swept sea
Surging into eternity.

— Ellen M. Carroll

The fickleness of the women I
love is only equalled by the
infernal constancy of the women
who love me.

— George Bernard Shaw

It's odd to think we might have been
Sun, moon and stars unto each other—
Only, I turned down one little street
As you went up another.

— Fanny Lee

Stephan's kiss was lost in jest,
Robin's lost in play,
But the kiss in Colin's eyes
Haunts me night and day.

— Sara Teasdale

Gentlemen always seem to
remember blondes.

— Anita Loos

Whom do we dub as Gentlemen?
The knave, the fool, the brute —
If they but own full tithe of gold,
and wear a courtly suit.

— *Eliza Cook*

When a woman like that whom
I've seen so much
All of a sudden drops out of touch,
Is always busy and never can
Spare you a moment, it means a Man.

— *Alice Miller*

I know I am but summer to your heart,
And not the full four seasons of the year.

— *Edna St. Vincent Millay*

I'd rather have two girls of 17
than one of 34.

—Fred Allen

Wedded she was some years,
and to a man
Of fifty,
and such husbands are in plenty;
And yet, I think,
instead of such a ONE,
'Twere better to have TWO of
five-and-twenty...
Ladies, even of the most uneasy
virtue,
Prefer a spouse whose
age is short of thirty.

—Lord Byron, Don Juan

In his younger days a man dreams of
possessing the heart of the
woman whom he loves; later, the
feeling that he possesses the
heart of a woman may be enough to
make him fall in love with her.

— Marcel Proust

54

Marriage may be compared to
a cage; the birds outside despair
to get in and those within
despair to get out.

— *Montaigne*

A husband is simply a lover with
a two-days' growth of beard...
and a bad cold in the head.

— *Dr. Louisa Duffe Booth*

A magician can saw a woman in half,
but it takes a husband to
make her go to pieces.

— *Jane Wilkie*

The truth has been staring us in the face for some 2,000 years: Men are forever on the lookout to have *affairs*...while the majority of women—even the seemingly most debauched of them— are eternally in search of love.

—Alexander King

If I had a pistol I would have shot him—either that or fallen at his feet. There is no middle way when one loves.

—Lady Troubridge

I want a girl just like the girl
that married dear old dad.

—William Dillon
(song lyrics)

A man looks pretty small at a
wedding, George. All those good
women standing shoulder to shoulder,
making sure that the
knot's tied in a mighty public way.

—Thornton Wilder
Our Town

Man's love is of man's life a
thing apart;
'Tis woman's whole existence.

— *Lord Byron*

Old men are like that, you know.
It makes them feel important to
think they're in love with somebody.

—*Willa Cather*

Youth had been a habit of hers
for so long, that
she could not part with it.

— *Rudyard Kipling*

From birth to age 18 a girl needs
good parents. From 18 to 35
she needs good looks. From 35 to
55 she needs a good
personality. From 55 on, she needs
good cash.

— *Sophie Tucker*

To men a man is but a mind.
Who cares what face he carries or
what form he wears? But woman's
body is the woman.

— *Ambrose Bierce*

She was a phantom of delight
When first she gleamed upon my sight;
A lovely apparition, sent
To be a moment's ornament.

— *William Wordsworth*

A woman is a dish for the gods.

— *William Shakespeare*

A man says what he knows,
a woman says what will please.

— *Jean Jacques Rousseau*

Man consists of body, mind and
imagination. His body is faulty,
his mind untrustworthy, but
his imagination has made him
remarkable. In some centuries,
his imagination has made life on
this planet an intense practice of
all lovelier energies.

— *John Masefield*